THIS
PAGE
LEFT
BLANK
INTENTIONALLY

The Policeman is My Friend

By Dr. Anthony T. Craft

The Policeman is My Friend

ISBN: 9798833964149

Independently Published

FOREWORD

The primary purpose of this book is to assist our precious children with beginning to know and respect the importance of law enforcement within our community. Our children need to know that police officers are here to help them and not to hurt them. Children need to be aware that police officers have families and loved ones and are quite capable of providing and conveying affection. Police Officers are human beings just as anyone else.

My overall purpose for composing this book stems from a conversation I recall engaging with the very respectable Minister Dr. Rosemary Smith Griffin, who speaks about her family and the love they share every day. As it relates to today, police officers are not respected as they were in the past. Mainly because of the screening process used to hire new officers. There's a different breed of police officer from this day forward.

ACKNOWLEDGEMENT

In these days and times, police officers are being provoked by a society who displays doubt, disgrace, disapproval, and degradation towards law enforcement and any form of authority. Politicians and legislators are fighting each other across the aisle, while nothing helpful towards our society is being accomplished. Police departments are busy searching for Luke-warm body counts to fill the missing slots of employment, instead of the professional-minded candidates who deserve their rightful chance.

There is little or no screening conducted before candidates are hired. Most, or many of the police departments hire prejudiced, racial, anti-social personalities who hide behind their badges and guns to show what power they have. We, as a society have got to start looking towards the future and concentrating on our children so that we can change to attitude of the world. That is the purpose of this children's book titled, "The Policeman is My Friend." We have got to get better when it comes to LOVE for one another. This is not a dog-eat-dog world unless that is what we make it to be.

I hope all children of the world can learn and see what the better side of living in the free world looks like. Let's hope and pray that GOD intervenes and get us back on-track. STAY BLESSED!

DEDICATION

This work is dedicated to my youngest brother, Brian Sherard Craft, who took his own life on January 12, 2020. Little did he know; he was that light at the end of the tunnel for many of the children at the school in which he was employed. He let them know that there was indeed a light there! There are times when people believe that they are trapped in their own deep hole with no relief in-sight.

BUT GOD HAS NEVER LEFT US!

Look Everybody, There's a Police Station!

Police Cars are Always Parked Outside the Police Station

The Policemen and Women Help to Keep Us Safe!

Don't Be Afraid of the Police Because They are Always Doing Their Job!

Policemen and Women are Always There to Assist Us!

FLAT TIRE

It's Great to Know the Policeman, the Policeman, the Policeman!

The Policeman's Job is to Keep Everyone Safe!

Police officers are your friends.
They want to help you.

Policemen Officers, Firemen and EMS Come to Help You When You Need it!

Policemen and Women Always Respect their Flag!

Policemen and Women Like it When You Speak to Them!

Have You Ever Spoke to a Policeman or Woman?

Make Sure You Shake a Policeman or Woman's Hand!

Wouldn't it Be Great to Become a Police Officer?

Oh! Look at the Police Hat, the Police Hat, the Police Hat

Oh! Look at the Police Hat, the Hat the Policemen and Women Wear?

Police hats come in all sizes. I Bet there's one that fits YOU TOO!

Oh! Look at the Police Car, the Police Car, the Police Car!

Oh! Look at the Police Car, the Car the Police Officers Drive

Don't be Afraid of Police Cars. All Police Cars Have Sirens, and Lights!

When You See and Hear Police Officers with Loud Sirens and Lights Flashing, they are On Their Way to Help Someone in Need!

Wouldn't it Be Great to Become a Police Officer?

Oh! Look at the Police Badge, the Police Badge, the Police Badge!

Police Badge

Sheriff Badge

Oh! Look at the Police Badge, the Badge the Policemen and Women Wear!

A good policeman keeps his badge shinny and bright!

Oh! Look at the Police Handcuffs, the Police Handcuffs, the Police Handcuffs, the Police Handcuffs!

Oh! Look at the Police Handcuffs, the Handcuffs a Policeman or Woman Carries!

Police Use Handcuffs When Bad Guys & Gals Get into Trouble!

Oh! Look at the Police Radio, the Police Radio, the Police Radio!

Oh! Look at the Police Radio, the Police Radio, the Policemen and Women Carry!

Policemen and Women Use Their Radios to Talk to Each Other!

Wouldn't it Be Great to Become a Police Officer?

The Policeman Tells the Cars When to Stop and Go!

The Policeman Works the Street, Catching All the Bad Guys!

You Can become a Policeman or Policewoman too!

The Policeman and Policewoman can make their whistle blow!

Some Policemen
and Women Come
with Dogs, So...

Wouldn't it Be Great to Become a Police Officer?

Have You Ever Seen a Police Dog?

MBK Labels

They are Called K-9's

Police Officers Keep Us Safe from Day to Day

Do You Feel Safe When the Police is Nearby?

If You See a Bad Guy, Tell Your Teacher Right Away!

Always Let Your Teacher and Parents Know Who the Bullies Are!

Policemen and Women Visits Our Schools!

Your Teacher Can Invite a Policeman or Woman to Your School!

Policemen and Women Go to Church on Sunday!

Policemen and Women Like to Listen to Music!

Policemen and Women Like to Sing Happy Songs!

Wouldn't it Be Great to Become a Police Officer?

Policemen and Women Love Spending Time with Their Families!

Policemen and Women Love and Cherish Little Children!

Policemen and Women Love to Eat Healthy Foods!

Policemen and Women Love to Visit the Gym

Policemen and Women Like to Study!

They Attend the Police Academy to Learn News Laws

Policemen and Women Always Obey the Rules!

Policemen and Women Listen to Their Mothers, Grandmothers, and Aunts!

You Should Obey Your Parents, and Teachers, always!

Policemen and Women Listen to Their Fathers

Listen to and Obey the Elders in Your Life

Go to Bed When You Are Told!

Eat All Your Vegetables!

Help Around the House with Cleaning!

Policemen and Women Always Protect Their Brothers and Sisters!

Share with Your Brothers and Sisters!

Try Your Best to Make Good Grades in School!

Wouldn't it Be Great to Become a Police Officer, Like My Friend?

YOUR PICTURE BELONGS HERE!

- ALWAYS BE THE BEST YOU THAT YOU CAN BE!

- WINNING DOESN'T ALWAYS MEAN BEING FIRST. IT MEANS YOU'RE DOING BETTER THAN YOU HAVE DONE BEFORE!

- DO THE RIGHT THING, EVEN WHEN NO ONE IS LOOKING!

- WHEREVER YOU GO, GO WITH ALL YOUR HEART!

- ALWAYS TRY TO BE A RAINBOW IN SOMEONE'S CLOUD!

-

- THE MORE YOU READ, THE MORE THINGS YOU WILL KNOW. THE MORE YOU LEARN, THE MORE PLACES IN LIFE YOU WILL GO!

THE END!

About Your Author

Hello, my name is Dr. Anthony T. Craft, and I am a retired veteran Law Enforcement Officer of twenty-five years. I am also a retired Master Sergeant (E-8) from the United States Army Reserves, after serving twenty-eight years. I earned my PhD. In Philosophy with a Specialization in General Psychology from Northcentral University in September of 2021. I am interested in enlightening our children about issues and concerns they may witness throughout their lives. All, in the form of children's books.

THIS

PAGE

LEFT

BLANK

INTENTIONALLY

Made in the USA
Las Vegas, NV
14 October 2022

57287884R10048